THE BEATLES for Kids

ISBN 978-1-4950-9602-0

HAL•LEONARD®
7777 W. BLUEMOUND RD. P.O. BOX 13819 MILWAUKEE, WI 53213

In Australia Contact:
Hal Leonard Australia Pty. Ltd.
4 Lentara Court
Cheltenham, Victoria, 3192 Australia
Email: ausadmin@halleonard.com.au

Visit Hal Leonard Online at
www.halleonard.com

THE BEATLES were an English rock band often considered to be the most influential music group of the rock era. The band's members were John Lennon, Paul McCartney, George Harrison and Ringo Starr. Their early rock and roll style became more innovative as they later explored many other styles and recording techniques, including pop ballads, folk-rock, Indian music, psychedelic styles, and hard rock. Each album released exhibited something new that set precedents for rock groups that followed. Often called the "Fab Four," "Beatlemania" aptly describes their enormous popularity as international stars. The group performed together until 1970, and after that continued music careers of their own. The Beatles remain the best-selling band in history.

ALL YOU NEED IS LOVE was written in 1967 for the BBC's global production *Our World*, which showcased live broadcasts from around the world. The song's strong message at a time of conflict immediately made it widely loved. Notice that eighth notes are to be played in Swing style (long-short). First learn the right hand alone. Next, look for the descending left hand pattern: G-F#-E starting in bar 4 and continuing throughout.

ALL MY LOVING was written in 1963. It was the first time Paul McCartney wrote the lyrics before he wrote the melody. This tune is moderately fast, and needs some energy to bring it to life. Have fun with the moving bass line in the left hand. Check out the left hand pattern in the first ending. You'll play that bass line again three more times. Can you find them all?

The distinctive two-bar introduction in **BLACKBIRD** sets the mood and the tempo. Carefully establish the quarter-note beat before playing. This is important because of the changing note values. In just the opening three bars you move from quarter note to half note to eighth notes to sixteenth notes. Be aware of accidentals; sharps, flats, and naturals not in the key signature. Practicing hands separately can help you identify these.

The happy vibe in **GOOD DAY SUNSHINE** comes from the easy swing feel of the eighth notes. Notice that in the opening syncopated rhythm, each lyric syllable is equal to three half beats, or three eighth notes. As you look through the song, you'll see many repeated sections and similarities. Once you've learned the first page, you'll be able to play the rest of the song easily.

HERE COMES THE SUN was written by George Harrison, and was recorded on the *Abbey Road* album. The signature riff in bars 14-15 (recurring four more times) could be counted in groups of three eighth notes: **1**-2-3, **1**-2-3, **1**-2-3, **1**-2-3, ending with 1-2-3-4. Each group of three begins with an accent. Practice the right hand first, and then add the left hand on all the accented eighth notes.

HEY JUDE was released as a single in 1968. Its simple character is illustrated with only three chords in the beginning: F, C and B♭. Practice the left hand alone to learn the shifts in position before trying hands together. You will see that many phrases are repeated, so the actual amount of music to learn is less than it appears. The coda is repeated many more times on the original recording. Feel free to repeat as you like.

I WANT TO HOLD YOUR HAND was The Beatles' best-selling single worldwide, released on the *Meet the Beatles* album in 1963. Lots of fun rhythmic motives make this song really rock. Right from the very beginning, the melody incorporates a groovy dotted-eighth-sixteenth figure that is repeated throughout the verse. Contrast this with the straight-eighth chromatic left hand riff in bars 2 and 6. Use the fingering given to play all the shifts easily.

IN MY LIFE opens with a lyrical introduction that appears again at the end of the song. Play this beautiful melody in a very legato style, connecting each note. It will be helpful to play right hand alone first, carefully noting the fingering. Take some extra time with bars 6-7 as you carefully count the sixteenth notes and practice moving the thumb from E to E♭.

LET IT BE was the last single released before its writer, Paul McCartney, announced that he was leaving the band. Play in a simple style, and with a bit of movement to keep from playing too slowly. The first four bars are repeated, and then you have a four-bar refrain, which is repeated at the end. So you really only have eight bars of music to learn in order to play this song easily.

LOVE ME DO was The Beatles' debut single in 1963. Have fun swinging the eighth notes! The first eight bars mimic the opening harmonica solo on the recording. You'll need only two chords, G7 and C, until the middle eight bars when the D chord joins in. Note the slanted lines moving from treble to bass and back to treble clef. This shows where the melody moves from hand to hand.

WITH A LITTLE HELP FROM MY FRIENDS was sung by drummer Ringo Starr on the *Sgt. Pepper's Lonely Hearts Club Band* album. The melody falls in a very limited range, enabling you to play the first two pages with only slight adjustments to your right-hand position. Play the melody with swing eighths (a long-short feel) as indicated. This tune is constructed from four-bar phrases that often repeat twice or more. Noticing this will help you learn the song quickly.

Once you've learned the first four bars of **YELLOW SUBMARINE**, you've learned most of the song. Even though "March" tempo is indicated at the beginning, be sure to swing the eighth notes for a bit of a bouncy vibe. This is a shortened version of the recording. Check out the original performance for more verses.

YESTERDAY is a beautiful, melancholy ballad. Look out for accidentals (sharps, flats, and naturals not in the key signature) throughout. Practice the melody with the fingering given. The melody spans over an octave, so you will need to shift your hand accordingly. You may choose to add pedal once you've learned the notes securely.

Another tune from the *Abbey Road* album, **OCTOPUS'S GARDEN** is written in cut time. This means that there are two half-note beats per measure. It can be counted in 4/4-time, but try to feel it in two beats per measure. Once your left hand has established a strong and steady beat, add the right hand. Practice the repeated 6ths in the right hand in bars 17-24, keeping your hand in the same shape for accuracy as you shift from 6th to 6th.

ALL YOU NEED IS LOVE

Words and Music by JOHN LENNON
and PAUL McCARTNEY

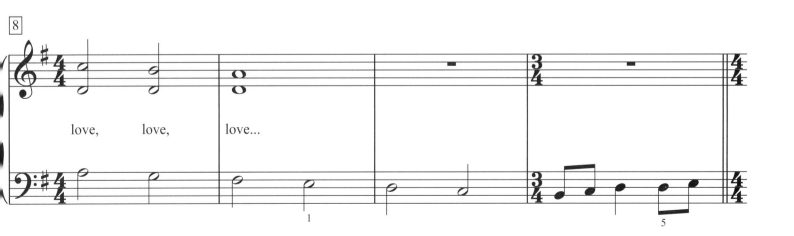

There's noth - ing you can do that can't be done.
Noth - ing you can make that can't be made.
Noth - ing you can know that is - n't known.

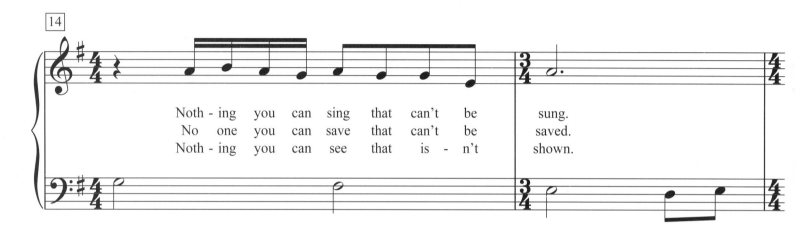

Noth - ing you can sing that can't be sung.
No one you can save that can't be saved.
Noth - ing you can see that is - n't shown.

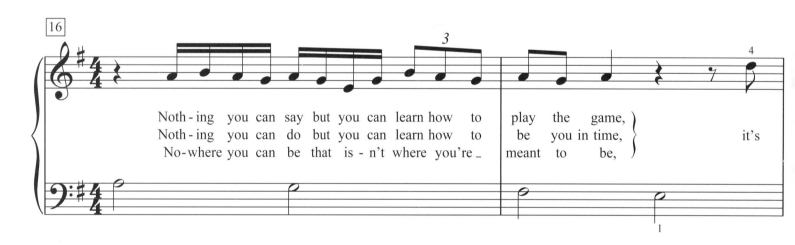

Noth - ing you can say but you can learn how to play the game, it's
Noth - ing you can do but you can learn how to be you in time,
No-where you can be that is - n't where you're _ meant to be,

eas - y.

All you need is love, all you need is

love, all you need is love, love,

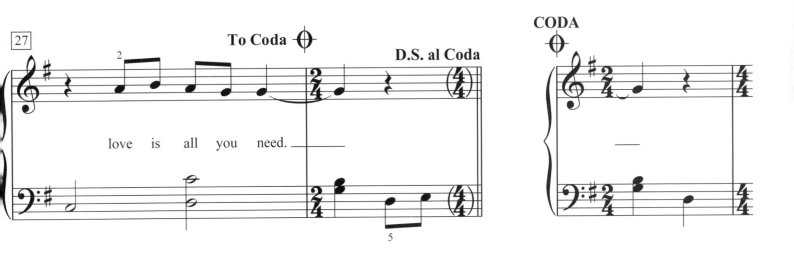

To Coda ⊕   **D.S. al Coda**   **CODA** ⊕

love is all you need.

Love is all you need.   Love is all you need.   Love is all you need.

ALL MY LOVING

Words and Music by JOHN LENNON
and PAUL McCARTNEY

Close your eyes and I'll kiss you, to-
tend that I'm kiss-ing to the

mor - row I'll miss you, re - mem - ber I'll
lips I am miss - ing and hope that my

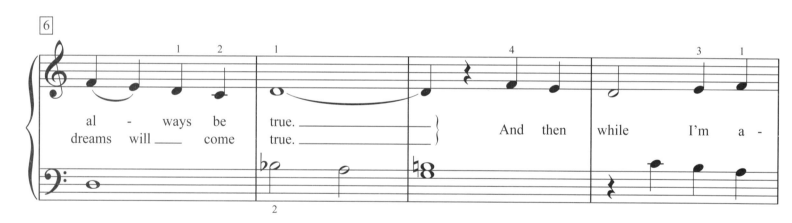

al - ways be true. _____
dreams will ___ come true. _____ And then while I'm a -

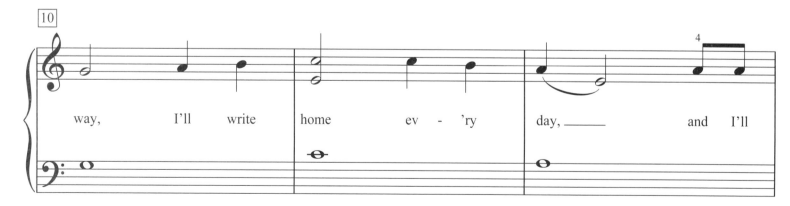

way, I'll write home ev - 'ry day, _____ and I'll

13 send all my lov - ing to you. ___ I'll pre -

17 2., 3. you. ___ All my lov - ing, I will send to

21 To Coda ⊕ you. ___ All my lov - ing, dar - ling, I'll be

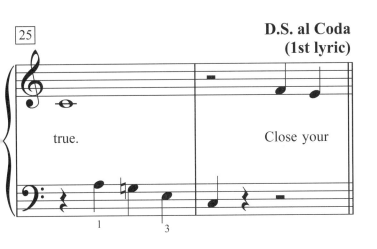

25 D.S. al Coda
(1st lyric) true. Close your

CODA
⊕ true. ___

BLACKBIRD

Words and Music by JOHN LENNON
and PAUL McCARTNEY

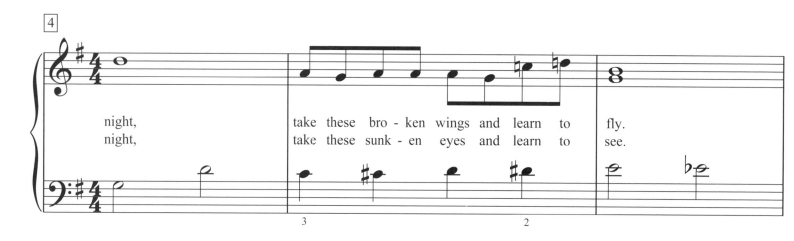

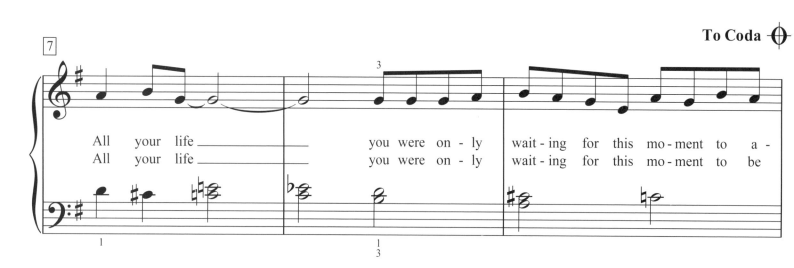

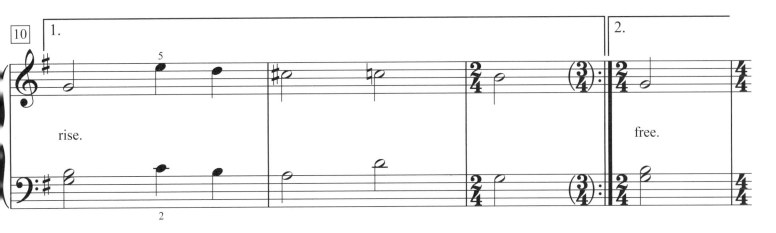

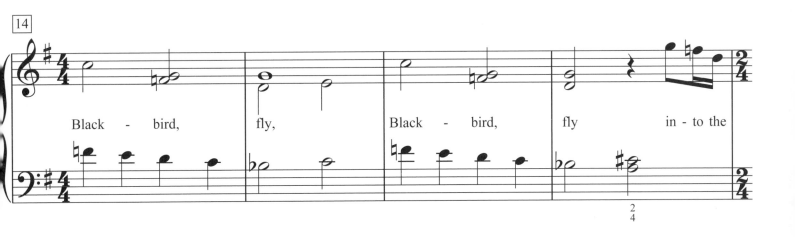

D.S. al Coda
(1st lyric)

CODA

GOOD DAY SUNSHINE

Words and Music by JOHN LENNON
and PAUL McCARTNEY

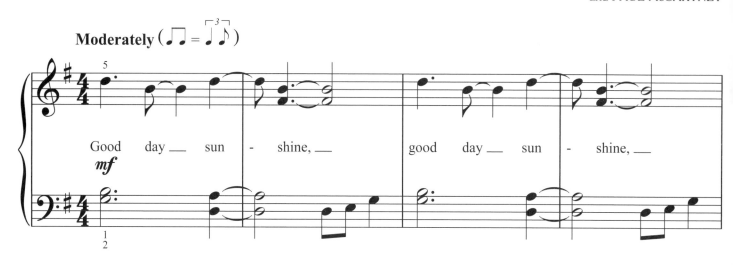

Good day _ sun - shine, _ good day _ sun - shine, _

good day _ sun - shine. {I need to laugh and when the
Then we'd lie be - neath a

sun is out, I've got some-thing I can laugh a - bout. _ I feel
shad - y tree, I love her _ and she's lov - ing me. _ She feels

good   in a | spe - cial way,   I'm in love, and it's a
good,   she knows she's | look - ing fine,   I'm so proud to know that

sun - ny day. __   Good day __ sun - shine, __   good day __ sun -
she is mine. _

To Coda ⊕

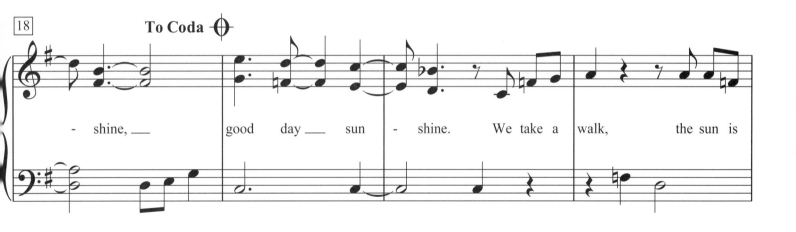

- shine, __   good day __ sun - shine. We take a | walk, the sun is

shin - ing down, | burns my feet as they | touch the ground.

25

D.C. al Coda

CODA

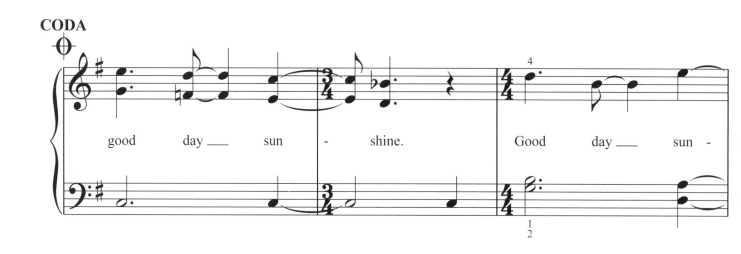

good day ___ sun - shine. Good day ___ sun -

32

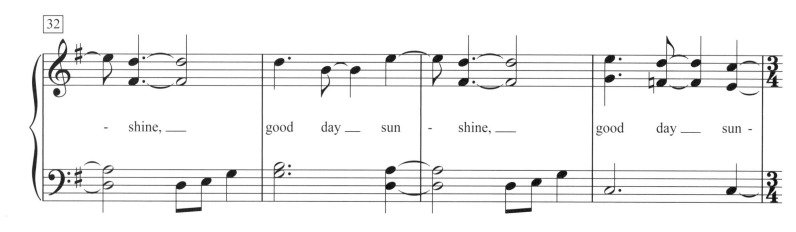

- shine, ___ good day ___ sun - shine, ___ good day ___ sun -

36

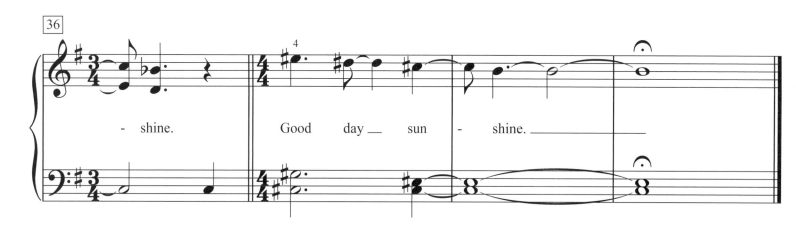

- shine. Good day ___ sun - shine. ___

HERE COMES THE SUN

Words and Music by
GEORGE HARRISON

Moderately

Here comes _ the sun, doo da doo doo. Here comes _ the

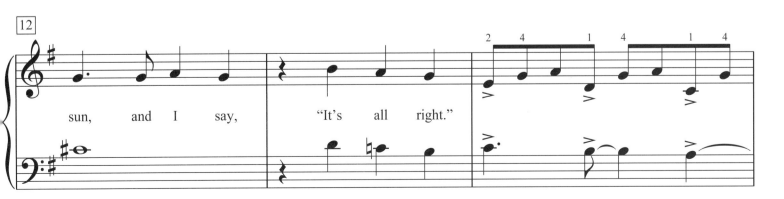

sun, and I say, "It's all right."

Lit - tle dar - ling, it's been a
Lit - tle dar - ling, the smiles re -
Lit - tle dar - ling, I feel the

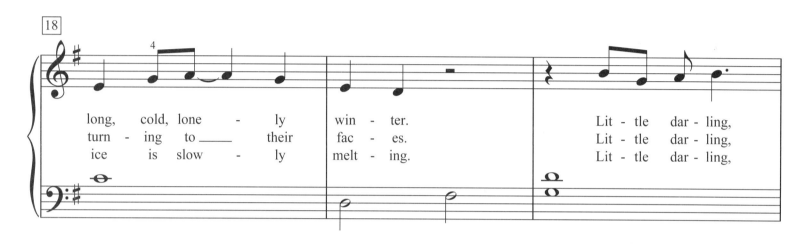

long, cold, lone - ly win - ter. Lit - tle dar - ling,
turn - ing to ___ their fac - es. Lit - tle dar - ling,
ice is slow - ly melt - ing. Lit - tle dar - ling,

it feels like years since it's ___ been here.
it seems like years since it's ___ been here.
it seems like years since it's ___ been clear.

Here comes ___ the sun, here comes ___ the

sun,   and I   say,   "It's   all   right."

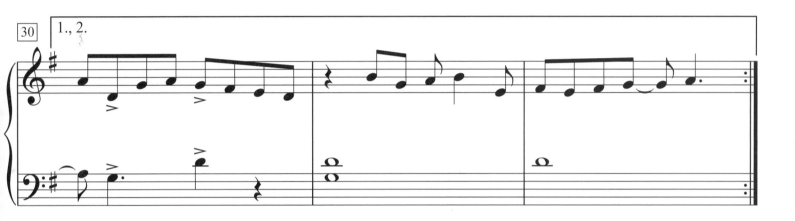

"It's   all   right."

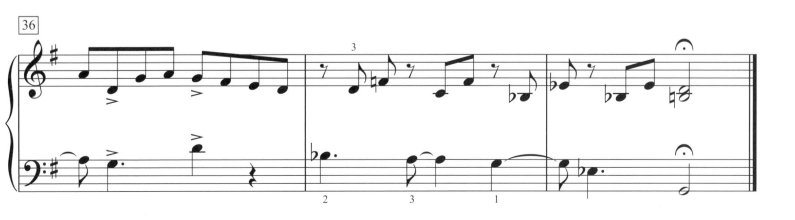

HEY JUDE

Words and Music by JOHN LENNON
and PAUL McCARTNEY

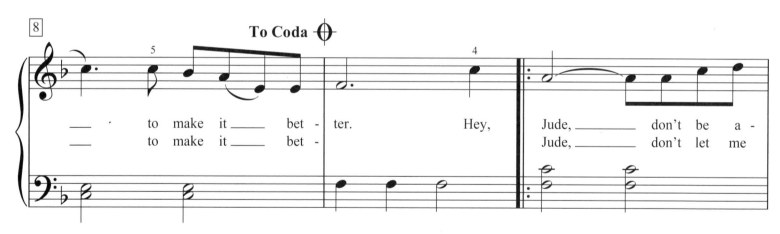

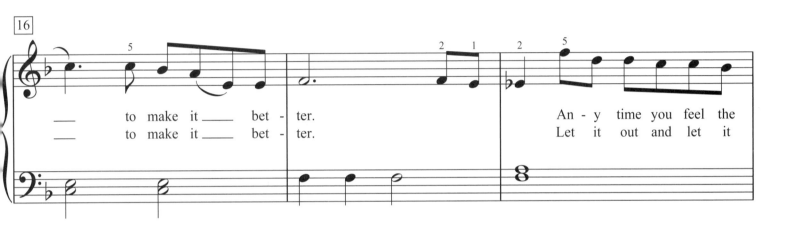

25

by mak - ing his world ___ a lit - tle cold - er. ___ } Da da
the move - ment you need ___ is on ___ your shoul - der. ___ }

28

1.

2. **D.S. al Coda**
(2nd lyric)

da da da da da da. Hey, Hey,

CODA

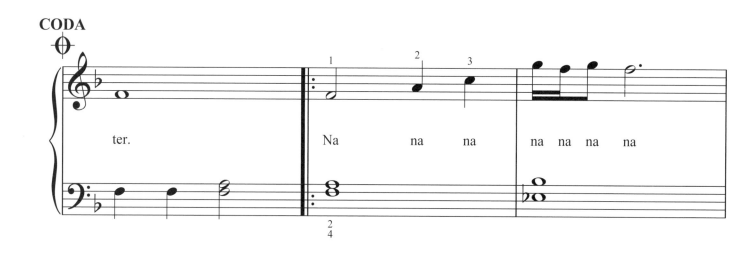

ter. Na na na na na na na

35

1. 2.

na na na na hey ___ Jude. Jude.

I WANT TO HOLD YOUR HAND

Words and Music by JOHN LENNON
and PAUL McCARTNEY

With a steady Rock beat

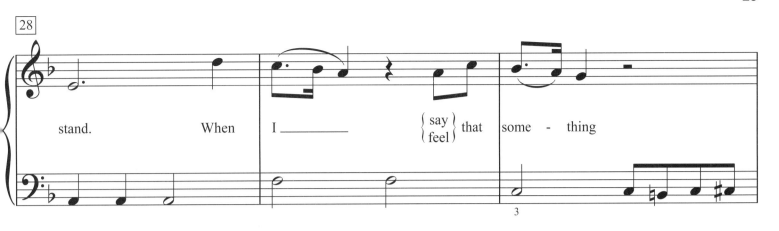

stand.   When   I _____ { say / feel } that some - thing

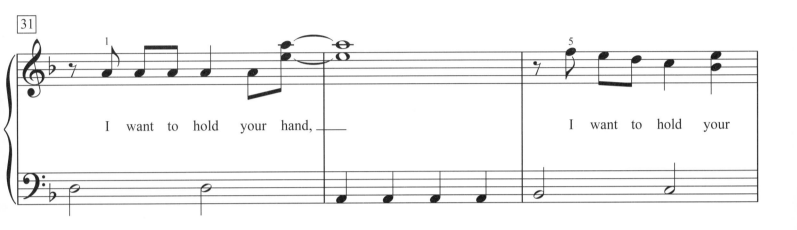

I want to hold your hand, _____   I want to hold your

hand, _____   **1.** I want to hold your hand.   **2.** I want to hold your

hand,   I want to hold your hand.

IN MY LIFE

Words and Music by JOHN LENNON
and PAUL McCARTNEY

Moderately

There are plac - es I'll re - mem - ber, all my
But of all these friends and lov - ers, all there is

life, _____ though some have changed, some for - ev - er, not for
no _____ one com - pares with you, and these mem - 'ries lose their

bet - ter, some have gone, _____ and some re - main. All these
mean - ing when I think of _ love as some - thing new. Though I

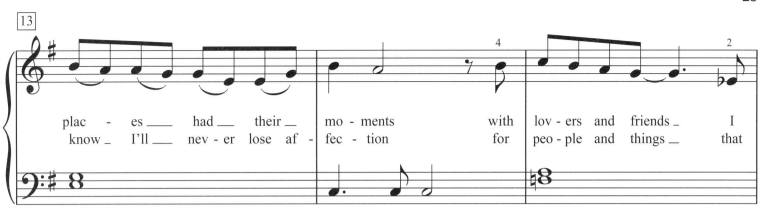

LET IT BE

Words and Music by JOHN LENNON
and PAUL McCARTNEY

Slowly

When I find my-self in times of trou-ble,
when the bro-ken heart-ed peo-ple

Moth-er Mar-y comes to me
liv-ing in the world a-gree,

speak-ing words of wis-dom; let it be. _____
there will be an an-swer, let it be. _____

And in my hour of dark-ness, she is
For though they may be part-ed there is

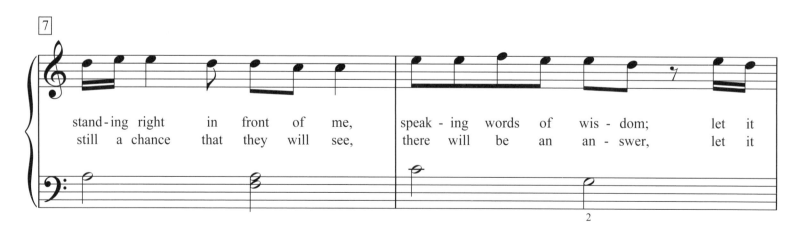

stand-ing right in front of me,
still a chance that they will see,

speak-ing words of wis-dom; let it
there will be an an-swer, let it

LOVE ME DO

Words and Music by JOHN LENNON
and PAUL McCARTNEY

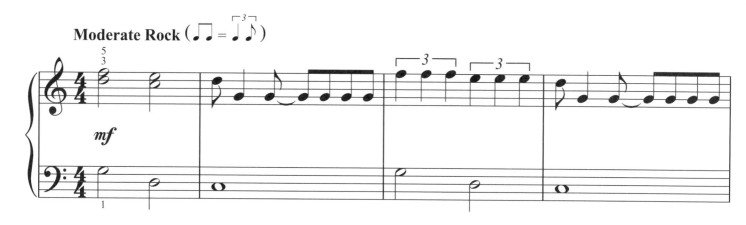

Love, love me do, ___ you know I love you, ___ I'll al - ways be true, ___

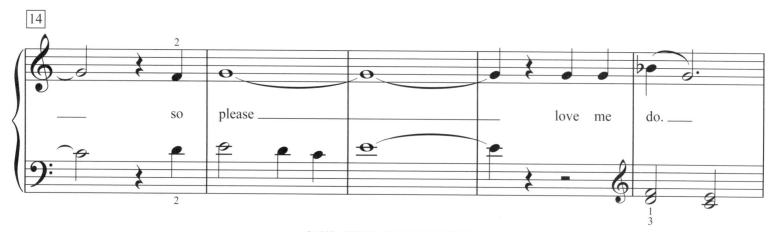

___ so please _____ love me do. ___

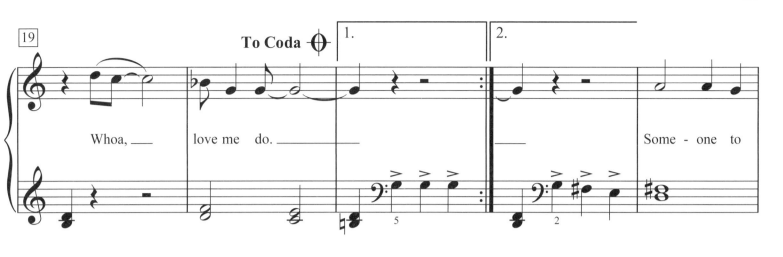

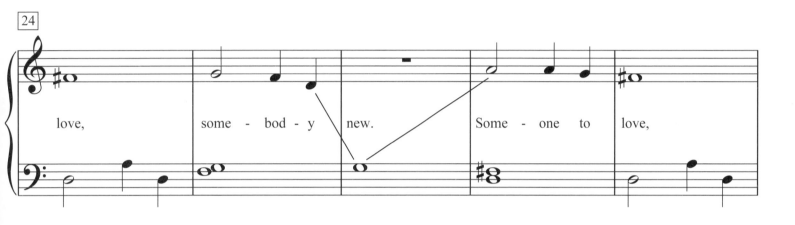

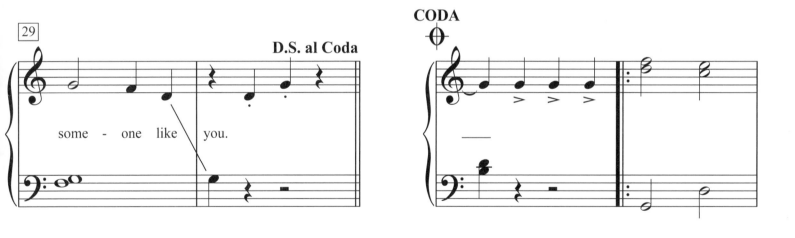

WITH A LITTLE HELP FROM MY FRIENDS

Words and Music by JOHN LENNON
and PAUL McCARTNEY

With a lilt

What would you do ___ if I sang ___ out of tune? ___ Would you stand ___
What do I do ___ when my love ___ is a - way? ___ Does it

___ up and walk ___ out on me? ___
wor - ry you to be ___ a - lone? ___

Lend me your ears ___ and I'll sing ___
How do I feel ___ by the end ___

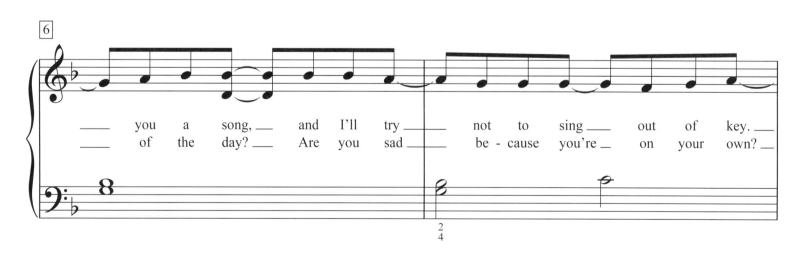

___ you a song, ___ and I'll try ___ not to sing ___ out of key.
___ of the day? ___ Are you sad ___ be - cause you're ___ on your own? ___

Oh,
No, I get by _____ with a lit-tle help ____ from my friends, _

____ oh, I get high ____ with a lit-tle help ____ from my friends, _

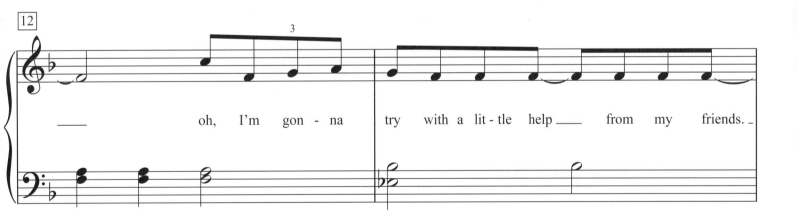

____ oh, I'm gon - na try with a lit-tle help ____ from my friends. _

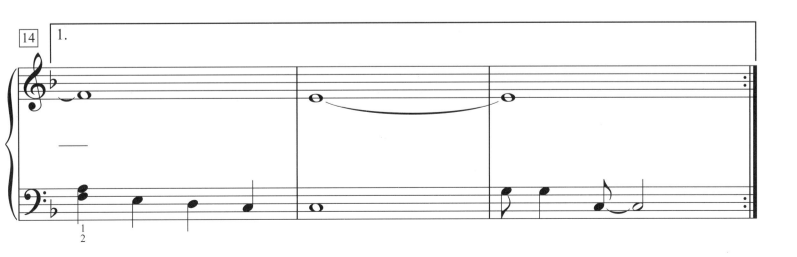

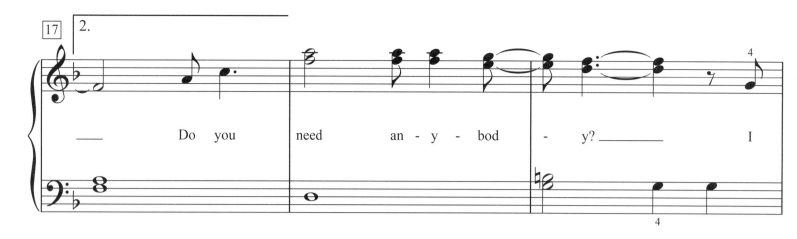

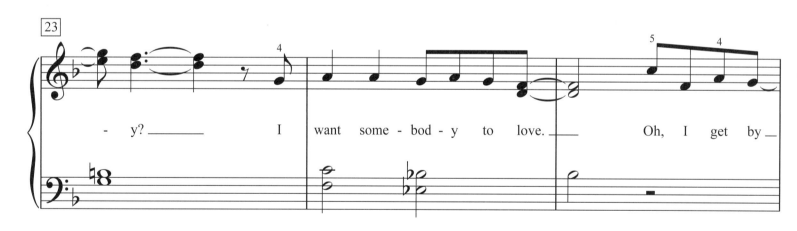

try with a lit-tle help ____ from my friends, ____ yes, I get high ____

____ with a lit-tle help ____ from my friends, ____ oh, I get by ____

____ with a lit-tle help ____ from my friends, ____ with a lit-tle help ____ from my friends! ____

YELLOW SUBMARINE

Words and Music by JOHN LENNON
and PAUL McCARTNEY

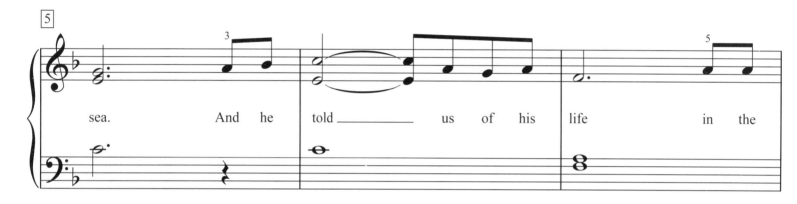

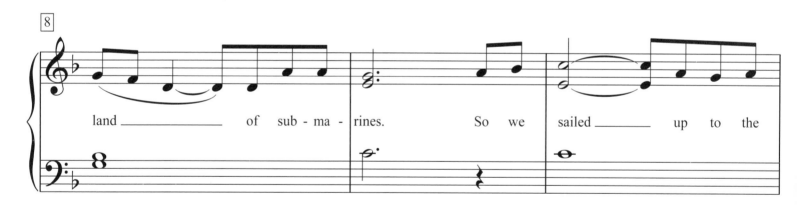

lived _____ be - neath the waves in our yel - low sub - ma -

rine. We all live in a yel - low sub - ma - rine,

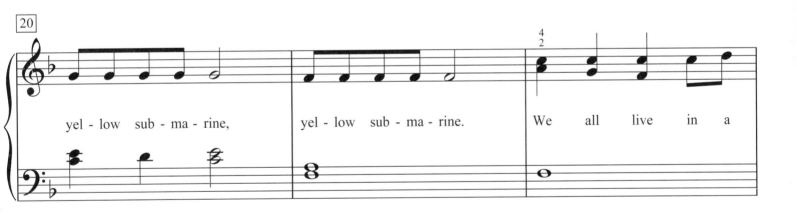

yel - low sub - ma - rine, yel - low sub - ma - rine. We all live in a

yel - low sub - ma - rine, yel - low sub - ma - rine, yel - low sub - ma - rine.

YESTERDAY

Words and Music by JOHN LENNON
and PAUL McCARTNEY

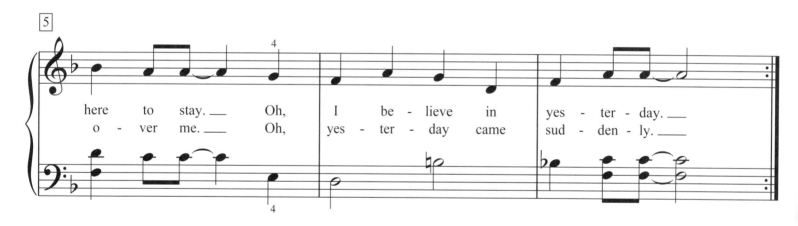

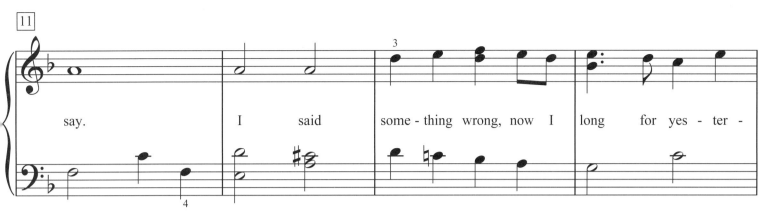

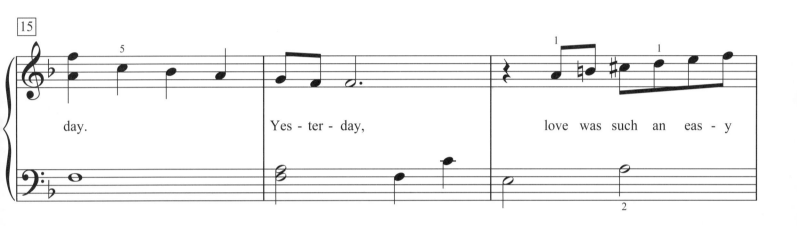

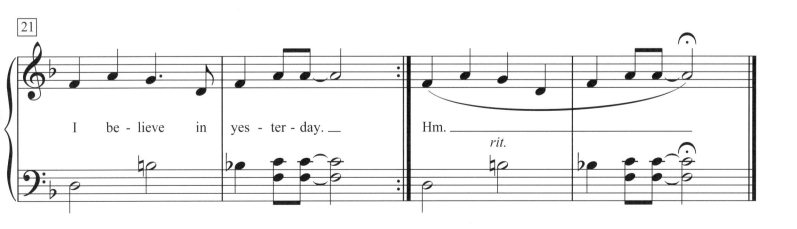

OCTOPUS'S GARDEN

Words and Music by
RICHARD STARKEY

Moderately

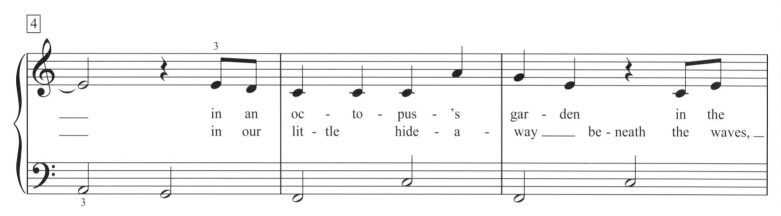

oc - to - pus - 's   gar - den   in the   shade.
oc - to - pus - 's   gar - den   near a   cave.

I'd   ask   my   friends   to
We would sing   and

come   and   see _____   an oc - to -
dance   a - round _____   be - cause we

pus - 's   gar - den with   me. _____
know   we   can't   be found.

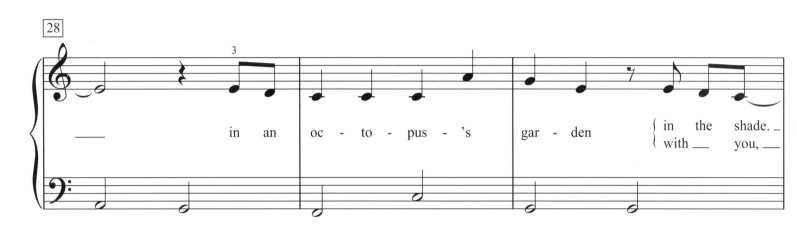

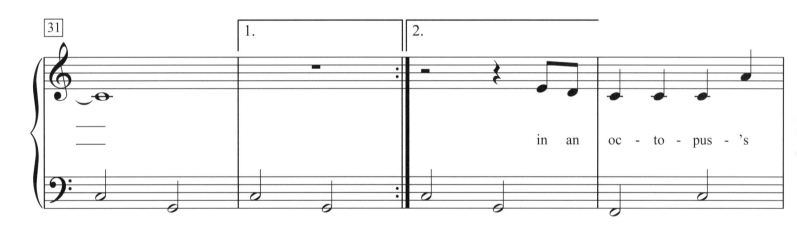

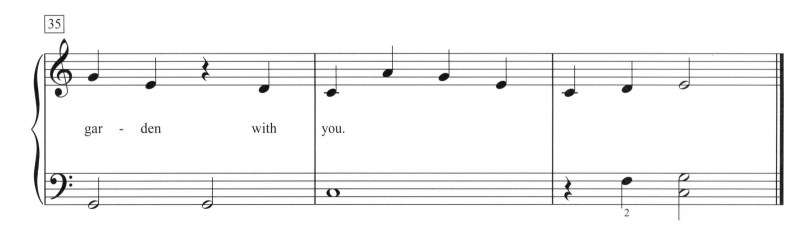